THE STORY OF
GEORGE WASHINGTON CARVER

Eva Moore

Illustrated with prints by Alexander Anderson
and with photographs

SCHOLASTIC INC.
New York Toronto London Auckland Sydney

Acknowledgments:
Historical Picture Service, Chicago, cover, pages 4, 93 (portrait); Prints Division, New York Public Library, Astor, Lenox and Tilden Foundations, pages 6, 11, 14, 18, 21, 24, 25, 37, 47, 49, 51, 56, 62, 68, 77, 87; The Bettmann Archive, pages 28 (bottom), 80, 84; George Washington Carver National Monument, Diamond, Missouri, pages 28 (top), 33, 38, 57, 74, 88; Culver Pictures, pages 63, 75, 93 (stamp); Polk's Studio, Tuskegee Institute, Alabama, pages 71, 95.

ISBN 0-590-42660-5

36 35 34 33 32 31 30 29 28 27   23/0

Printed in the U.S.A.   40

THE STORY OF
GEORGE
WASHINGTON
CARVER

George Washington Carver was the son of a slave. No one knows for sure what day he was born, or even what year. Dr. Carver thought he was born about 1864. Some people think he may have been born in 1859 or 1860. This picture was taken when Dr. Carver was a college student. He was about twenty-six years old.

One

IT WAS WINTER in the town of Diamond Grove, Missouri, in the year 1864. It was a dark, cold night and Moses Carver couldn't sleep. Suddenly he heard a sound outside, far away but coming closer. It was the sound of horses galloping fast. He jumped out of bed and began to get dressed.

Moses Carver had to hurry. He knew that the men who were riding these horses were robbers — robbers who stole slaves. Moses Carver had a slave, a woman named Mary. She and her two little boys lived across the road in a log cabin. Mary took care of the children herself. Their father was dead.

Moses Carver was afraid the night riders would steal Mary and her children. Night after night he listened for the sound of horses' hoofs beating on the road. Whenever he heard it, he got up and took Mary to a secret hide-out.

It was the time of the Civil War, when the states in the North and the states in the South were fighting each other. One reason they were fighting was because of slaves.

Many farmers in the South had slaves to work on their farms and in their houses. The slaves were black people who were made to work without pay.

The first slaves had been taken from their homes in Africa and brought to America on big ships. They were sold on the slave market. From then on

they belonged to another person, and so did their children. In Africa they had been free people. Now they were somebody's property.

On big cotton farms, called plantations, there were thousands of slaves. The man who owned the plantation owned the slaves. They had to do what he told them. If they didn't, or if they tried to run away, they could be beaten — or even killed.

It was against the law to have slaves in the North. Many people in the Northern states thought that slavery should be against the law everywhere in the country. But farmers in the South would not set their slaves free. And so the two parts of the country were at war.

Most of Missouri was fighting on the side of the North. But in the very southern part of the state — where Moses Carver lived — slavery was allowed. The people who lived there were fighting on the side of the South.

Moses Carver hoped the North would win the war. Even though he had a slave, he knew that slavery was wrong. He had always taken good care of Mary and her children. He did not want the night riders to get them.

The night riders stole slaves in Missouri and sold them to plantation owners in Arkansas and other states in the South. What would happen to Mary if she was captured and sent into the cotton fields to work? Moses Carver could not bear the thought of such a cruel life for Mary.

That winter night when he heard the riders far off, Moses ran across the road to the log cabin where Mary lived. He heard the horses coming closer and closer. He knocked on Mary's door and called to her, "Do you hear? They are coming again! Hurry!"

Mary opened the door. She was holding a baby in her arms. The baby was crying.

"Oh, Uncle Moses," Mary said, "my little George is so sick. I can't leave him here."

The sound of horses' hoofs grew louder and louder.

"Quick! Take him to the hide-out," Moses said. "I'll get Jim." He ran to a cot where a little boy was sleeping. He picked the child up and ran out the door. Mary went out after him. The baby cried and cried.

"He'll be cold," Mary thought, and she went back inside to get a blanket. When she came running out, the horses were there. She ran to get away, but the riders were too fast. One of them grabbed her by the arm and pulled her onto his horse. With her other arm, Mary held her baby close. She cried out, "Help! Uncle Moses, help!"

Moses Carver heard Mary's cries, and then he heard the horses gallop away into the dark night.

The next day, Moses went into town. He was looking for a man named Bentley. He had heard that Bentley would go after stolen slaves, if you paid him enough. Moses did not want Mary to die in the cotton fields. He would pay Bentley well to bring her and the baby back.

"If you find them," Moses Carver said to Bentley, "I will give you forty acres of my best timberland."

The man didn't say anything.

"And," Moses Carver added, "I will give you my fastest horse, Pacer."

Bentley shook Moses Carver's hand. "It's a deal," he said.

Seven days later, Bentley rode up to the Carver's farm — without Mary.

"I followed their trail into Arkansas," the man told Moses and his wife. "No sign of the girl. This is all I found." He held out a dirty blanket. Inside was Mary's baby — small, still, hardly breathing.

"I guess I can't take full pay for a sick baby," Bentley said. "I'll just take Pacer."

Moses Carver went to the stable to get the horse. His wife held the baby close and she thought about Mary.

"Poor Mary," she whispered, and she looked at the baby. "Poor child. What's to become of you?"

Two

MARY'S BABY George was sick for a long time. Mrs. Carver was afraid he was going to die. She fed him, nursed him, and rocked him to sleep. Every day he got a little stronger.

As the years passed, George grew very slowly. When he was seven years old, he was skinny and small for his age. He looked like a brown baby bird, all head and eyes. His voice was as high as a bird's, and he stuttered when he talked. He was often sick.

His brother Jim, who was three years older, was stronger. Moses Carver took Jim out to the corn fields to work, and little George helped Mrs. Carver around the house.

The Civil War was over now, and it was against the law for anyone to own slaves. Moses Carver told Jim and George that they were free. This meant that they could leave if they wanted to. The boys did not want to go. This was the only home they had. And they loved the Carvers and called them "Aunt Susan" and "Uncle Moses."

Because George could not do much work, he had a lot of time to himself. He liked to walk in the woods and listen to the birds. He liked to lie on the damp ground and watch the tiny worlds of insects. He liked to touch the plants that grew wild among the trees.

"All the living things!" he thought. "Where do they come from? Why are they here? What makes them live and grow?"

In a little while, George began to notice that some plants are strong and some are weak, just like people. He felt sorry for the weak and dying flowers he saw in Aunt Susan's garden. Why should they die when the others were so strong? George looked closely at the strong plants to see what was different about them.

The little boy grew to love all the flowers in Aunt Susan's garden. He liked to put his cheek against the soft petals of the roses. Once Jim came by and saw George bending over a rose bush.

"What are you doing to those flowers?" Jim asked.

"Loving them," said George.

George began to understand more and more about plants. He took care of Aunt Susan's garden, and all the flowers grew bigger and stronger.

One day a lady came to see Aunt Susan. It was Mrs. Baynham, who lived in a big house down the road. She had a garden too.

"What beautiful roses you have!" she said to Aunt Susan. "I can never grow roses like that. How do you do it?"

"I don't do anything," Aunt Susan said. "It's our George. He's the one who knows about roses."

Mrs. Baynham wanted George to go to her house and look at her garden. Maybe he could tell her how to make her roses bloom.

When they got there, George looked around him and his heart sank. Poor roses! Mrs. Baynham had planted her garden too close to the trees.

"Please m-move them, ma'am," he said to Mrs. Baynham. "T-take them out of the shade. They'll die here. R-roses want s-sun."

Mrs. Baynham planted her rose bushes in the sun, and soon they began to bloom. She told everyone in town how Carver's George had saved her garden. People began to come to the Carver's farm and ask George what to do about their sick plants. In Diamond Grove, seven-year-old George was known as The Plant Doctor.

Three

GEORGE had other things to do besides take care of plants. He helped Uncle Moses and Jim plant corn. He fed the chickens and the horses. He helped Aunt Susan with the housework.

The Carvers lived in a big one-room house on their farm. In one part of the house were two wide beds. George and his brother Jim slept together in one of them. In another part of the house was a long, cross-legged table with four stools around it. Every evening, George set the table himself, putting down a pretty blue- and pink-flowered dish at each place.

A spinning wheel was near the fireplace in the house. George's mother Mary had once used it to do the spinning. Now it was Aunt Susan who worked it, spinning cotton into yarn.

On days when George was not feeling well he would stay inside with Aunt Susan and make things. He liked to work with his hands. He had a small knife and he used it to whittle little shapes out of wood. He kept all of them in a box.

He learned how to knit and crochet by watching Aunt Susan. "I can do that," he said to himself, and he made his own knitting needles from two turkey feathers.

Sometimes George would sit by the fire and read the book Aunt Susan had given him. It was a spelling book, a little blue book with long lists of words in it. Aunt Susan told him what most of the words were. There were a lot of words that George had never heard, and he didn't know what they meant.

George wanted to know. He wanted to know a lot of things. He wanted to go to school. But in Diamond Grove, Missouri, there was no school for George.

When George was eight years old and wanting to go to school, there was a law in Missouri that said white children and black children could not go to the same school. And the only school in Diamond Grove was for white children. The nearest school for black children was in the town of Neosho, eight miles away.

George told Aunt Susan about his wish to go to school. "What do you need school for?" she said. "You know more than most of those school children already."

George spent more and more time taking care of plants. He had a secret garden in the woods where he grew plants and flowers. It was a kind of plant hospital. When George found a dying plant, he would pull it up gently by its roots and plant it in his secret garden. He talked to the plant as he patted dirt around its roots.

There was so much George wanted to learn about plants — and about other things too.

One day George went to see how Mrs. Baynham's roses were growing. He walked through the

sunny garden, touching each soft rose. All at once he found himself at the front door of Mrs. Baynham's house.

George had never been inside the house. It was one of the biggest houses in the town. George had heard that Mrs. Baynham had rugs on the floor, pictures on the wall, and books — a whole bookcase full.

Without really thinking about what he was doing, George walked up to the door and pushed it open. He wanted to see those books.

Inside, the house was dim and quiet. George took a few steps. The rug under his feet felt as soft as a carpet of moss.

The first thing George saw were two big pictures hanging over the fireplace — pictures of a man and a woman. Both of them were dressed in fancy clothes with lace at the neck. George thought they were beautiful. He was looking so hard at the pictures that he did not hear Mrs. Baynham come in.

"Why, George!" Her voice made George jump. "What are you doing here?"

George pointed to the pictures. "What are th-those?" he asked.

"They are paintings, of course," Mrs. Baynham told him.

"How do you d-do it?" George wanted to know.

Mrs. Baynham liked to talk about her pictures. "Well, first the artist makes his colors. And then he dips the brush in, and then he paints the shapes he wants."

George began to understand. "You mean, s-somebody made these with his h-hands?"

Mrs. Baynham nodded yes.

George forgot about asking to see her books. He wanted to get home and make a painting himself. As soon as he left the house, he picked a bunch of red pokeberries that grew along the road.

When he got home, George squeezed the fat pokeberries until he had a dish full of deep red berry juice. Now he had a color to paint with, but what could he paint on?

In the barnyard, George found a flat rock. He dipped his finger into the juice and began to draw on the rock. He did not try to draw a man or a woman. He drew flowers. He drew until he had filled the rock with swirls of red flowers.

From then on George thought that next to taking care of flowers, the most wonderful thing in the world was to paint them.

Four

On Sunday, most people in Diamond Grove went to church. But Uncle Moses stayed home. He worked on Sundays, the same as he did every day. He took Jim with him, and they spent all day out in the fields.

George was curious about church. Whenever he could get away from the farm on Sunday mornings, he would walk to the pretty church and sit on the steps. The sound of the minister's voice came through the closed door, and George sat as still as he could trying to hear the words. Most of the time he couldn't understand anything. But it wasn't the talking he came for anyway.

Every now and then the minister would stop talking and everyone would sing. The voices were loud and strong, and George could hear them perfectly. This is what he waited for every Sunday. It was the singing that he liked.

George liked to sing too. In a soft, high voice he would try to sing along with the people inside the church. And he sang other times, when he was walking through the woods or doing his work. The only time George didn't stutter was when he was singing.

After a while, people began to notice George sitting on the church steps every week. One Sunday, Mrs. Baynham had news for him.

"If you like church so much, George," she said, "you should go to Sunday school. I just talked with the minister, and he says you can go if you want. You can start next Sunday."

George could hardly believe his ears. A school, right in the church! A school for him.

But after the first day, George knew that Sunday school was not the kind of school he dreamed of. In Sunday school he heard stories about Noah, and Jonah, and Joseph. But he didn't learn what made snow and hail. He didn't learn whether or not he could change the color of a flower by changing its seed. These were the things he wanted to know most of all.

Now George was ten years old, older than most of the children in the Sunday school. They all went to regular school too. "If they can, why can't I?" he wondered.

More and more George thought about the school for black children in Neosho, eight miles away. "If we lived in Neosho," he thought, "then I could go to school. Maybe Jim would take me there to live."

But Jim did not want to leave Uncle Moses and Aunt Susan and the farm in Diamond Grove. "What do we need school for?" he said. "We have a good life here. Besides, Uncle Moses would never let us go."

"Yes, h-he would!" George said. "He said we are f-free. We can go when we want."

The next day, George told Aunt Susan and Uncle Moses that he was going to Neosho. He was going to school.

"Do you really want to go?" Aunt Susan asked him. "All by yourself?"

George nodded. Nobody could make him change his mind.

On the day George left, Aunt Susan made corn bread. She cut it into pieces and stuffed each piece with some bacon and wild onion. These were corn dodgers for George to eat on his way. They were his favorite food.

When Aunt Susan gave the corn dodgers to George, she smiled. She was sure that after he had eaten them all and it grew dark outside, George would come hurrying home.

There were only a few things George wanted to take with him — his box of wood carvings and some pretty rocks he had found in the woods. He tied them up in a handkerchief.

George took one last walk in the woods. He stopped at his secret garden and bent over his plants and flowers. "Good-by," he whispered. Then he set out for Neosho.

Five

GEORGE KNEW which road went to Neosho. Uncle Moses used to take him and Jim there once a year. They rode in Uncle Moses' wagon then. Now George walked all the way.

It was getting dark when George came to town. He would have to hurry and find a place to spend the night. He headed for the part of town where black people lived.

George passed some little wooden shacks. He could not stay in any of these — people lived in them. Then he saw a big barn. Some of the boards were hanging loose. Some were missing. George peeked inside and he saw stalls — stalls for horses. And they were all empty.

George was tired from his long walk. He lay down in one of the dark stalls. How hungry he was! He wished he had not eaten all of the corn dodgers.

Outside George could hear the whippoorwills calling, "Whip poor will, whip poor will." The sound made George feel sad, and a little afraid. "Why did I ever leave home?" he asked himself. "What am I going to do in this strange place all by myself?" But George did not lie awake for long. He was too tired. He fell asleep.

In the morning, George was more hungry than ever. He found some berries and some wild clover to eat. That wasn't enough. George climbed onto a pile of wood and sat down. He tried to stop feeling hungry, but all he could think about was the good breakfast Aunt Susan would be cooking right then. He was almost ready to start walking back to Diamond Grove.

"Hey, there — you, boy!" A woman came out of the shack across the yard. "What are you doing on my wood pile?" the woman asked.

George felt like running away. He was too afraid to say anything.

The woman came closer. She was small, but she looked very strong. There was a friendly look in her eyes. George did not feel afraid any more.

"You're new here, aren't you?" the woman asked.

"Y-yes, ma'am," George answered. "I just c-came yesterday — from Diamond G-grove."

"Where's your ma and pa?" the woman wanted to know.

"Don't have a m-ma or pa," George told her. "I'm alone. C-came to go to s-school."

The woman smiled. "It's too early for school," she said, "but it's just the right time for breakfast. Come on in, and I'll see what I can find for your breakfast — if you're hungry, that is."

The woman's name was Mariah Watkins. She and her husband Andy did not have any children of their own. When they found out that George was alone, they were glad to take him into their home. Soon George was calling them "Aunt Mariah" and "Uncle Andy."

Just over the fence from the Watkins' house was an old log cabin. This was the Lincoln School, a school for black children set up by the

Mariah Watkins took George into her home and loved him as if he were her son. George always called her "Aunt Mariah."

Next door to Aunt Mariah's house was a school for black children where ten-year-old George became a pupil. The schoolhouse was a log cabin. It may have looked like the school in this old drawing.

United States government. It had one room. George sat on a wooden bench, elbow to elbow with other boys. There were over seventy children in the room. But George didn't care how crowded it was. He had a slate to write on and a book to read. And he had a last name.

All the children were given last names. George had been called "Carver's George" all his life. Now everyone called him George Carver.

After school, George helped around the house. Aunt Mariah was away sometimes, taking care of newborn babies. Then George would do the housework.

Aunt Mariah showed him how to cook a few things so he could make meals for Uncle Andy when she was away. And she showed George how to wash clothes in the big laundry tub outside. He helped her hang the clothes up to dry.

George wanted to give Aunt Mariah a garden. He found some wild orchids growing in the woods and he planted them near the fence.

Every Sunday, Aunt Mariah and Uncle Andy took George with them to the African Methodist Church. Now George could hear the talking part of church, and he grew to like it almost as much as the singing part. He wanted to be just like the minister when he grew up.

As soon as he had learned how to read well, Aunt Mariah gave him a Bible. George read to her and Uncle Andy every night.

In school George had learned how to read and write, how to add and subtract. But he wanted to know much more. The teacher taught the children everything he could. But he couldn't teach things he didn't know, and George was always asking questions the teacher could not answer.

One Saturday, George went to visit Jim and the Carvers. He told them about school, and about Aunt Mariah and Uncle Andy. The Carvers were glad that he had found such a good home. Jim began to think that he was missing something.

When George made the trip back to Neosho, he was not alone. Jim was with him. Now he was going to be a pupil in Lincoln School, like his little brother.

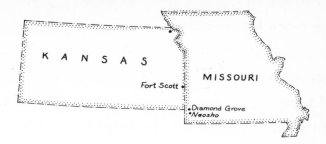

Six

GEORGE's brother did not stay in school long. He didn't like reading, writing, and arithmetic. But he did like the people in Neosho, so he stayed there and went to work.

George still went to school, even though he had learned everything the teacher could teach him.

One day George heard that some neighbors were going to leave Neosho and travel far away — to a place called Fort Scott in the state of Kansas. Fort Scott was a bigger town than Neosho, and there was probably a free school there. George wished he could go. In a new school, there would be a new teacher — maybe one who knew about snow and hail and flowers.

The neighbors liked George. They told him he could go with them if he could find a place to sit in their loaded wagon.

Before George left, he and Jim went to see the Carvers. George was afraid he might never come back and he wanted to say good-by to Aunt Susan and Uncle Moses. The traveling picture-taker was there, and the boys had their picture taken together.

Back in Neosho, George packed his bag. He put in the Bible Aunt Mariah had given him, and the little blue spelling book from Aunt Susan. He put in the box with his rocks and wood carvings — there were over five hundred little wooden shapes.

It was hard to say good-by to Aunt Mariah and Uncle Andy. For a minute, George wished he wasn't going away. But the wagon was there, waiting for him. It was loaded with pots and pans and furniture.

George climbed up and found a good place to sit. He looked so small, more like a little brown bird than a thirteen-year-old boy.

"I'll write l-letters!" he called as the wagon started down the road.

George was about thirteen years old when he and his big brother Jim had their picture taken together in Diamond Grove. Soon after, George left for Fort Scott, Kansas. He never saw his brother again. Jim died of smallpox six years later when George was still far away in Kansas.

Aunt Mariah and Uncle Andy and Jim waved. They could hardly keep from crying. Then they turned around and walked sadly home.

When he got to Fort Scott, George needed to find a job right away. But what kind of job could he get? He was not strong enough to do outdoor work. And people who needed someone for house-work wanted girls. When George tried to get a house job, he was turned down again and again.

Then he went to see a woman named Mrs. Payne. She had put an ad in the newspaper for a girl, but she talked to George anyway.

"Can you cook?" she asked him.

George thought of the simple meals he had made for Uncle Andy. That was all the cooking he knew how to do. But he needed this job, and all he said was, "Yes, ma'am."

"Good!" Mrs. Payne clapped her hands. "You can cook Mr. Payne's dinner tonight. Let's see . . . I think we'll have honey-baked ham and sweet potatoes, biscuits, pudding, and coffee."

George swallowed hard. He had never baked a ham before. He had never made biscuits, or pudding. But if he told Mrs. Payne he couldn't make these things, he would never get the job. Suddenly he had an idea.

"Yes, ma'am," he said. "But I want to make everything j-just the way you l-like it. If you could just s-show me your way of f-fixing everything . . ."

"Of course," Mrs. Payne said. She showed him how much honey she put on the ham. She showed him how she mixed the biscuits and the pudding. She never knew that she was really showing George how to cook everything. Mr. Payne liked his dinner, and George got the job.

Before long George learned to cook other dishes. Soon he was inventing his own recipes. Mr. Payne thought he was the best cook in Fort Scott.

In Fort Scott, there was no one to take care of George. He had to look after himself. He had to earn money to buy his meals and to rent a room to sleep in. He had to work so much of the time that he could not go to school very often.

When he did go to school, George learned fast. He could go through one grade twice as fast as other boys.

George was small and quiet, and most people were kind to him. But some white people would pick on him or make fun of him when they saw him in the street — just because he was black. The Carvers had given George a good home. Other white people, too, had been good to him. But he knew that many white people did not like any blacks.

George did not know why. The Bible said it was wrong to hate another person — hate was a sin. And a sin was a weakness in the eyes of God.

Then one summer day, something terrible happened in Fort Scott. A mob of white men and women murdered a black man, and George saw everything they did. They dragged the man out of the city jail, beat him, and killed him right on the street. Their faces were full of hate. George never wanted to see those faces again. The next day, he left Fort Scott for good.

Seven

GEORGE went to another town in Kansas. Then he went to another, and another, and another. He stopped in any town where there was a school, and where he could find work. Some of the schools George went to were just for blacks. Some were for both black and white children. George learned everything he could in each school, and then he moved on. He was sure that some day he would finish all the grades. He knew what he would do then. He would go to college.

As he traveled from town to town, George was always alone. He saved enough money to buy an accordion, and he taught himself to play it. Music made him feel less lonely.

George traveled from town to town, making his way through school. In one of the towns, George had his picture taken in a photographer's studio. He was probably fifteen or sixteen years old.

When George came to the town of Olathe, Kansas, he went to the Presbyterian Church. There he met a man named Christopher Seymour and his wife Lucy. They made him think of Uncle Andy and Aunt Mariah. When the Seymours invited George to stay with them, George knew he had found a new home, a new aunt and uncle to love.

Aunt Lucy Seymour had a laundry business, and people brought their clothes to her to be washed and ironed. George wanted to help her. He was so good with his hands that soon he could iron as well as Aunt Lucy. He would spend half a day pressing a lady's dress so it would be just right.

George was good at games too. Uncle Chris taught him to play checkers. When George began to win all the time, Uncle Chris was sorry he had such a good pupil.

Now George did not have to work all the time, and he went to school every day. In one year, he went through the fifth and sixth grades. George was older than most of the other school boys, but he looked as young as they. He had not grown very much since he left Neosho when he was thirteen.

George made friends at school and in church. He played his accordion in school concerts. He and his friends liked to put on plays. Being in plays helped George to stop stuttering so much.

After George finished sixth grade, Uncle Chris got a job in the town of Minneapolis, Kansas, and the Seymours moved there. They took George with them on the train. Even though George was over sixteen, he was so small that he only had to buy a child's ticket.

Then, in just one year, George did enough growing to make up for all the years of being small. He grew to be six feet tall. But his voice did not change. He had a high, clear singing voice, and people liked to hear him sing. But it seemed strange to hear such a sweet, tiny voice coming from such a tall, grown-up man.

Now George was a young man, and he thought it was time he had a place of his own. He found a small house with one room and a little kitchen built onto it. Instead of steps going up to the door, the steps went down because the house was below street level. George moved into this little house. He bought a wash tub, an ironing board, and an iron, and he opened his own laundry.

George had learned everything the school in Minneapolis could teach him. He thought he was ready for college. He began to write letters to different colleges, asking if they would take him as a student.

George looked for the mail every day. Some days the mailman left him letters addressed to George Carver — but the letters were not for him. There was another George Carver in town, and George was getting that man's mail.

George wanted to be sure to get his own mail. He decided to make his name different by adding a middle initial. He went down the alphabet, trying different initials until he came to "W." George W. Carver — that sounded good.

George's friends thought the "W" should stand for a real middle name. "How about Washington?" one of them said as a joke. "George Washington."

George thought it over. "Might as well be Washington as be W.," he said. Soon all his friends were calling him George Washington Carver.

Eight

ONE DAY the mailman left a letter at George's house. The letter was addressed to him — George W. Carver. It was from Highland College, in Highland, Kansas. This was one of the schools George had written to.

George ripped the envelope open. Would Highland take him as a student? He let the envelope drop to the floor as he opened the letter. Yes! The letter said yes, he could come to Highland in the fall and sign up for classes.

George did a little dance of joy. He was going to college at last.

Highland was far away from Minneapolis, and George would need money for the train ride. He had a little money saved. If he could sell his laundry tub, his iron, and ironing board, he would have enough money for the train ticket. He was sure he could get a job in Highland, and pay the college after he had earned some more money.

That September, Aunt Lucy and Uncle Chris went to the train station with George. As the train came into the station, George could see people sitting in the cars. Most of the people were white, and they were sitting on big soft seats that looked like armchairs. In one car, George saw black faces looking out of cracked or broken windows. This was the "Jim Crow" car for Negroes. Blacks could not ride in the cars with white people.

George kissed Aunt Lucy good-by and climbed into the Jim Crow car. He was on his way.

For most people in the Jim Crow car, the ride was not comfortable. There were no soft armchair seats, just hard wooden benches. But George hardly felt the bumps as the train skipped over the rails. In his pocket was the letter that said he was going to be a college student. He felt as if he were living in a dream.

When the train got to Highland, George went right to the college. He asked to see the head of the school.

"What do you want?" the man asked as George walked into his office.

"I'm George W. Carver, sir." George pulled the letter out of his pocket. "You wrote to me. I am here to begin college."

The man did not look at the letter. "I'm sorry," he said to George, "there has been a mistake. We do not take Negroes here. If I had known you were colored, I would not have asked you to come."

George felt tears come into his eyes. He walked out of the office and into the sunny street, trying to blink away the tears. He had never felt so sad and so angry. He knew that the man was not really sorry. This man did not care how hard George had worked to come to Highland. All that mattered to him was the color of George's skin.

Now what would George do? He wanted to run

away, to get as far away from this town as he could. But he did not have much money left. He would have to stay.

George went looking for work. After a while, some people he did housework for learned what had happened at the college. They were sorry for George, and they wanted to give him extra money. But George would not take even a nickel. "I will not take any money that I don't earn," he told his friends.

One of the men George worked for told George about his son, who had a big farm in western Kansas. "The government is giving away land out there," he said. "My son has to live on his land and farm it for five years — and then it is his, free and clear. You could do it too."

George liked the idea of having a farm of his own. And here was a way to get land even though he didn't have much money.

In 1886, when George was twenty-two, he moved out west and tried to start a farm. It was hard work. Western Kansas was like a desert. It was hot, and the land was dry and sandy.

George thought the desert flowers were beautiful. He grew many kinds of cactus, but most of the crops he planted would not grow. In two years, George knew he could not make a living here. He found someone to take over his farm and he moved east again.

Nine

GEORGE TRAVELED for three months. First he went east, and then he headed north. He worked in towns along the way, doing any job he could find. He washed clothes, he ran errands, he pitched hay, he took care of horses. He always hoped that, in some town, he would find a job in a greenhouse where he could take care of plants.

When he got to the town of Winterset, Iowa, he decided to settle down for the winter. The regular cook in the Schultz Hotel was away for a few months, and George took his place.

In Winterset, George went to the Methodist Church. He was the only Negro there, but no one told him to leave. George went to church every Sunday. When the people sang hymns, he sang too.

One Sunday, a man came up to George after church. "I am Dr. John Milholland," he said. "My wife and I think you have the best singing voice in this church. Would you come to our house and sing for us someday?"

George visited the Milhollands often. They became good friends. Mrs. Milholland had a little greenhouse in the backyard. George helped her grow orchids and petunias in the greenhouse.

Mrs. Milholland also liked to paint. She let George use her paints and brushes. George thought he would be happy if he could spend his life painting pictures of the flowers he loved.

After a while, the regular cook at the hotel came back, and George was out of a job. But not for long. With Dr. Milholland's help, he rented a little house and opened a laundry business.

George's house was near the end of town, next

to a woods. Every morning before he started to work, George picked up a basket and went walking in the woods. When he found a weed or a leaf he had never seen before, he put it in his basket. Later he would go to the library and try to find out what kind of plant it came from.

"George is running his own school," Mrs. Milholland said. "He is the teacher, and the pupil too."

The Milhollands knew that George had once tried to go to college. They thought he should try again.

"Anyone who wants to know as much as you do belongs in college," Mrs. Milholland said. "And you have talent. You might even become a fine painter if you could get the right teacher."

"But where could I go?" George said. "Where is there a college that would take me — a Negro?"

"There is a school not far from here," Dr. Milholland said, "Simpson College. They once had a Negro student. I'm sure they would take you."

Dr. Milholland was right. On September 9, 1890, George became the second black student at Simpson College. All the other students in his class were sixteen or seventeen years old — George was twenty-six. All the other students were happy and excited to be starting college. But no one was as happy or as excited as George Washington Carver.

Ten

GEORGE wrote letters to the Milhollands from Simpson. In one letter he wrote,

"The people are very kind to me here and the students are wonderfully good. They took it into their heads I was working too hard and had not enough home comforts, so they clubbed together and bought me a whole set of furniture — chairs, table, bed, and such things as I needed."

George had many friends at Simpson. The younger students liked to take walks in the woods with him. He told them about every plant, every kind of rock. As they walked in the woods, they heard birds singing. "Listen," George would say, "that's a chickadee." He could tell any bird by the song it sang, even when he could not see it. No teacher was as interesting to the students as their friend George.

George opened a laundry to earn money. He was busy all the time. He read his lessons while he scrubbed clothes. He read some more as he ate his lunch. Sometimes some friends would come to visit, and George would go on reading and working while he talked with them.

The class George liked most of all was art class. His art teacher, Miss Budd, thought he was a very good painter. And she knew how much he loved to paint. But she knew, too, that it was hard for even the best artists to make money. It would be harder — maybe even impossible — for a black artist to make a living. She told George what she thought.

"Your paintings are beautiful, George. But artists die poor. Isn't there something else you would like to do? You know so much about growing things — maybe you should change to science. You would be doing work you enjoy, and still make a good living."

George wanted very much to be a painter. But he knew Miss Budd was right. And he began to think about his place in the world. He had been hurt many times because he was a black. Yet he knew that other blacks were not as lucky as he. Most of his people were poor and poorly educated. Worst of all, they had no hope. If he became a scientist or a teacher, maybe he could help his people. Maybe he could do something that would give them hope for a better life.

Miss Budd wanted to help George. "My father is a science teacher at the Iowa State College," she

George Washington Carver's love for learning led him from Diamond Grove, Missouri, to Ames, Iowa — with many stops in between.

told him. "It is a very good school. You could learn every kind of science there. If you want me to, I will write to Father and ask him to get you into Iowa State College for the summer term."

George had been at Simpson College for less than a year. In May, 1891, he moved to the town of Ames, Iowa, fifty miles away. He began to study at Iowa State College.

Iowa State was a bigger college than Simpson. It was a college of *agriculture*. Most of the students were there to learn the best ways to grow crops and to raise cattle and other livestock. They had to learn a lot of science. George signed up for science classes — geology, botany, chemistry, zoology.

George was a popular student at Iowa State. The students and the teachers liked him. But one thing really bothered George. He was not allowed to eat with his friends in the dining room. He was told to have his meals with the field hands down in the basement.

George wrote to a friend of his at Simpson, Mrs. Liston. He told her how bad this made him feel.

Mrs. Liston came to visit him right away. At lunch time, she was invited to eat with the students and teachers in the dining room. But she would not leave George. She went down to the basement and ate with him and the field hands.

After that, George's friends felt ashamed. They did not care what the rules were. They wanted George to eat with them in the dining room, and he did.

The more George learned in college, the more he wished all his people could learn. Many black people in the South were farmers, but they knew little or nothing about the soil and how to grow good crops.

"If I can teach farmers how to make better farms," George thought, "I will be doing something good for my people."

He wrote to Mrs. Milholland:

"I am taking better care of myself than I have before. I realize that God has work for me to do, and I must be careful of my health."

Eleven

GEORGE liked painting too much to give it up altogether. When winter vacation came, he went back to Simpson and took more art lessons with Miss Budd. He liked to paint nature scenes and pictures of flowers and fruits. Sometimes when he was working on a picture, he put down the brush and painted with his fingers.

In 1892, George took four of his paintings to an art show in the city of Cedar Rapids. All four were chosen for the State Fair Art Show to be held in the spring. George could afford to send only one to the State Fair. He sent the one he liked best — a large painting of a desert yucca, a plant he had seen when he lived in western Kansas.

When he was a college student, George worked hard to become a good artist. He liked to paint flowers most of all. This painting was hung in a special art show. Three other pictures George had painted were also in the show.

During the last years of college, George became an expert in the science of animals — zoology, and in the science of plants — botany. He passed all the tests and was graduated in 1894. He was the first black to be graduated from Iowa State. Then he was hired to work at the college in the botany laboratory, and he was the first black on the college staff.

George spent two years working in the botany laboratory at Iowa State. In the laboratory he made experiments with plants, trying different ways to make them grow bigger and better. He took long walks in the woods, looking for plants that had a *fungus* — a kind of plant disease. He took these plants back to the laboratory and studied them under a microscope. He found hundreds of different kinds of fungus.

George wrote a paper about plant diseases, and it was printed in a booklet put out by the college and sent to scientists. The head of the Agriculture Department, Dr. James Wilson, thought that George knew more about plants and animals than anyone else at Iowa State College. He asked

George to go with him when he gave talks at science meetings.

George liked to make speeches about his work. He did not stutter any more. On the stage, he talked the same way he talked to his friends who used to walk with him in the woods. And, like his friends, the audience listened to every word.

George was a tall young man, but his shoulders were stooped from bending over so much — bending over laundry tubs, bending over flower gardens, bending over wild plants in the woods, bending over a microscope in the laboratory. His stooping shoulders and his high little voice made him seem older than thirty-two.

George never paid much attention to his clothes. Sometimes he wore the same suit day after day. But every day he wore a different wild flower in the buttonhole of his jacket.

At the age of thirty-two, George Washington Carver was not a famous man. But his work was known to small groups of scientists and teachers. One of the teachers who heard of George was Booker T. Washington.

George knew of Booker T. Washington too. He was the head of a school in the state of Alabama. The school was Tuskegee Normal School. It was a kind of college, and it was for black people.

On April 1, 1896, George got a letter from Booker T. Washington. Mr. Washington wanted him to come to Tuskegee, to be a teacher and to start a new department at the school — an agriculture department. George would be teaching young black farmers about soil and plants and farming. It was what he wanted to do.

George sat down and wrote his answer to Booker T. Washington. He said, "It has always been the one great ideal of my life to be of the greatest good to the greatest number of my people; and to this end I have been preparing myself these many years. I feel that this line of education is the key to unlock the golden door of freedom to our people."

George Washington Carver packed his bags again. He packed the little blue spelling book from Aunt Susan Carver. He packed his Bible from Aunt Mariah Watkins. He packed all the little wood carvings he had whittled when he was a small boy, and the knife he had whittled them with. He packed the brand-new microscope that the teachers and students of Iowa State gave him as a going-away present.

While George packed his treasures, he felt a little sad. They made him think of friends he had loved and left behind. Now he was going to a new place where he would make new friends, a new place where he was needed most of all.

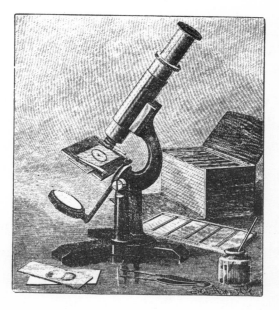

Twelve

Tᴜsᴋᴇɢᴇᴇ Normal School was in Macon County, Alabama. George took the train to the nearest railway stop, a few miles away from the school. Two students met him with a wagon.

As they drove along, George looked around him at the countryside. The soil was sandy, and near the banks of the river, it was mixed with red and yellow clay. George wished he could hop out of the wagon and look closely at the soil, and at all the strange plants he saw.

As they rode along, George saw cotton fields everywhere. He saw old, gray wooden shacks that looked as if they would not stand up in a strong wind. He knew that these were the homes of black farmers.

To him, these farmers were still slaves. They were slaves to the cotton crops they grew.

Long before the Civil War, the South had grown cotton. Cotton brought in a lot of money, and so farmers planted most of their land with cotton crops. But cotton crops were not good for the soil. They used up *nitrogen* — a gas that plants

On his way to Tuskegee, George may have seen farmers like these picking cotton.

need to grow. When the nitrogen in soil is used up, the soil cannot grow healthy plants.

Like many scientists, George was worried about the soil. If cotton crops destroyed the soil, what would happen to the farmers?

George thought it was time for farmers of the South to stop growing just cotton. He knew that most of them grew cotton because they didn't know how to grow anything else, and they were afraid to try. One thing he wanted to do at Tuskegee was to teach students about the soil — how to care for it, and how to grow crops that would not be harmful to the soil the way cotton was.

The wagon took George through the town of Tuskegee. The school was a mile away.

This school was different from Iowa State. There were no beautiful lawns — just acres of dirt. The buildings at Iowa State were pretty brick buildings. At Tuskegee, there was only one brick building. All the rest were built of wood. Some were not even painted. George could see that there was a lot of work to do.

There was no special building for students who wanted to study agriculture. Booker T. Washington had just raised enough money to buy the materials. The agriculture building was going to be a brick building. The students themselves would make the bricks and build it.

One of George's first jobs was to plan the building — classrooms on the first floor, a reading room and a plant room on the second, and a dairy in the basement.

George had thirteen students that first year. They called him Dr. Carver. Dr. Carver's class had a classroom, but they did not have a laboratory or tools to work with. The students were discouraged, but Dr. Carver would not let them mope around and do nothing.

"There's no need to whine *'Oh, if I only had so-and-so!'*" he said. "Do it anyhow. Use what you find around you."

And Dr. Carver took his students out to find anything that would be of use in a laboratory — old bottles and jars, boxes, pieces of string, rubber, tin, and wire. They searched through garbage cans and dump lots. Soon they had a homemade laboratory in the corner of the classroom.

Dr. Carver set up a farm on the school grounds

so that his students could practice working with the soil. Twenty acres of land were marked out in small plots. Dr. Carver called this farm an Experiment Station. He planned to do experiments in growing crops.

The soil of the Experiment Station was not very good. It would be hard to grow anything in this soil. Dr. Carver thought of two ways to make it better — put fertilizer in it, and plant crops that would add nitrogen.

Dr. Carver knew that waste materials would make a good fertilizer and would not cost anything. He asked his students to clear a piece of land and build a fence around it. He told them to put any kind of waste they could find into this pen — waste paper, garbage, rags. He told them to put in cut grass, leaves, and manure too. Then the students put some rich soil from the woods and swamps on the waste pile. When it had all rotted, they spread it on the plowed land.

Now the land was ready for planting. The students thought they would be planting cotton. But Dr. Carver said no — they would plant cowpeas instead.

Cowpeas, he told them, are *legumes*. So are beans and sweet peas and peanuts. These legumes grow in pods. They take nitrogen from the air, and give it out through their roots as they grow. And so legumes are good for the soil. Later some other crop can be planted in the same soil, and there will be plenty of nitrogen to help the new plants grow.

The leaves and flowers of the peanut plant grow above the earth. The roots and the pods grow underground.

Thirteen

Dr. Carver was a popular teacher. More and more students wanted to study agriculture. At the end of the first year, there were seventy-three boys and three girls altogether.

Dr. Carver wanted his students to learn the names of every plant and insect they saw. This was hard work. If a student found a plant or insect he could not name, he brought it to Dr. Carver. Dr. Carver always knew what it was. Some of his students began to bring in strange plants just to test Dr. Carver.

One day some boys thought of a joke to play on their teacher. They caught an ant, a beetle, a spider, and a moth. They used parts of each bug to make up a funny-looking insect.

"I think we have found a rare bug," they told Dr. Carver. "What is it?"

Dr. Carver looked at the strange insect for a few seconds. "Well," he said, "I think this is what is called a *humbug*."

The boys laughed at Dr. Carver's joke. He was too smart. They would not try to fool *him* any more.

Dr. Carver thought that all the students at Tuskegee should work hard to make the land around the school beautiful. He helped them plant grass and flowers, and he marked out walking paths so no one would trample the new lawn.

In the fall of 1897, a year after Dr. Carver came to Tuskegee, the brick agriculture building was opened. The students were not the only ones to use it. Every month farmers in Macon County came to the school for meetings. Dr. Carver would tell them about the soil.

"When the soil is like this" — he held up a handful of dirt — "it is ready for plowing. But if it sticks to the plow, then it's too wet. The air cannot get in, and the plant won't have anything to feed on unless it gets air."

Dr. Carver told the farmers how important it was to grow legumes. And he thought it was just as important for everyone to have a vegetable garden. Then they would not have to spend money for vegetables at the market. With the money saved, they could buy a hog or two — and have meat to last all winter long.

The farmers had a good time at the meetings. They sang hymns, and Dr. Carver read to them from the Bible and led them in prayers. Besides the lessons in farming, he gave lessons in cooking and sewing. Tuskegee was a busy place. George Washington Carver had a lot of work to do.

The students at Tuskegee helped to build the school's church. This photograph was taken about 1910.

Fourteen

THE SECOND YEAR, Dr. Carver's class planted sweet potatoes on the school farm. He thought that every farmer should have a sweet potato patch. Sweet potatoes were easy to grow, and they were good for the soil. They did not use up much nitrogen. Dr. Carver showed his students the right way to plow and how to plant sweet potatoes.

Another year, when the soil was good enough, Dr. Carver's students planted cotton on the farm. It was the best cotton crop they had ever seen.

Dr. Carver wanted all the farmers in Macon County to know about the good crops they were growing at Tuskegee. He wrote booklets about each crop. In a few years, farmers all over the county were learning how to grow bigger and better crops because of the work George Washington Carver and his students were doing, and because of the booklets he wrote for them.

But what of all the farmers who could not read? Dr. Carver thought of a way to help them too. On weekends, he loaded a cart with sweet potatoes, cowpeas, and other crops his students had raised on the school farm. He drove off to visit poor farmers in Macon County. When he showed them the samples, he told them how they could grow foods like this and, at the same time, make their soil better for growing cotton.

Dr. Carver always felt sad when he saw something going to waste. He told the farmers he visited to use everything nature gave them. There were vegetables and fruits growing wild in their backyards. These plants were good to eat. He showed the women how to make wild crab apples into jelly and catsup. Wild pumpkin could be dried and used as food all winter.

Many farmers thought that plants growing wild could not be worth much.

"Everything that helps to fill the dinner pail is valuable," Dr. Carver told them.

Sometimes Dr. Carver had some vegetable seeds to give the farmers. "Plant a garden, a little place by the house," he said. "But if you cannot afford to put a fence around it, don't have it where the chickens can get in and dig it up."

Dr. Carver showed the farmers how to make a kind of yellow paint out of Alabama clay. They could use it to paint their shabby houses and make them more cheerful. He showed the women how to make rugs by weaving dried okra stalks together, and how to crochet pretty mats for the table out of string.

Some of the farmers did not trust Dr. Carver at first. They thought he came to see them just to show off. But once they knew him, they could see he cared about them and wanted to help. The farmers welcomed Dr. Carver to their homes.

In 1906, Tuskegee was given money to build a new kind of school — a school on wheels. This school would go out to farmers and teach them as Dr. Carver had been doing. Dr. Carver drew a picture of how he thought the new school on wheels should be made. He drew a big wagon with shelves to hold tools, boxes of seeds, and bags of fertilizer.

Soon the school on wheels was ready to roll. Now more farmers could learn how to make better farms and have happier lives.

Dr. Carver's drawing was used as the model for Tuskegee's school on wheels. The wagon was named after Morris K. Jesup, the man who gave money to have it built.

Fifteen

By the time Dr. Carver had been at Tuskegee ten years, the school had changed. More students came, more buildings were built, more teachers were hired. By 1906, there were a hundred and fifty-six teachers, eighty-three buildings, and there were fifteen hundred students. More people were

In 1909, a new agriculture building was built. Now Dr. Carver and his students had a real laboratory to work in.

hearing about the school, and about the teacher and farm expert, George Washington Carver.

Groups of black farmers began to invite Dr. Carver to speak at their meetings. His students thought he should dress up when he was going to give a speech. But Dr. Carver didn't care what he wore.

"Are you going to wear that old suit?" his students would say as he was about to leave.

"I thought the people wanted to see *me*," Dr. Carver answered. "If they want to see suits, they can come to my room and I'll show them two or three."

After a while, Dr. Carver had so much to do that he had to give up teaching. But he liked to be with young people. He held a Bible class for the students every Sunday after dinner. He read his favorite verses to them and talked about God and nature.

Sometimes Dr. Carver held a special nature class for young children. He thought that every child should have a little garden of his own, and a small animal to take care of.

Once, a little boy brought Dr. Carver a present

— a fluffy baby bird he had taken from its nest in the woods.

Dr. Carver took the bird and held it in his big hand. He asked the boy to sit down, and he told him all about the bird — what kind of food it ate, and how it would look when it grew up. He whistled the song the bird would sing when it was bigger.

"Now take it back and turn it loose, my boy," Dr. Carver said. "Take it back to its mother. It is terrible when a young bird is taken from its mother."

"The first thing to know about a sweet potato," Dr. Carver said, "is that it is a morning glory." And that is just what the flower of this sweet potato plant looks like.

Sixteen

D R. CARVER spent many hours every day in his laboratory. He locked the door so that no one could come in and disturb him.

Some of the other teachers at Tuskegee did not like this. What was he being so secret about? He acted so strange, they thought, not at all like a teacher should. But the head of the school, Booker T. Washington, believed in him. He let Dr. Carver do his work the way he wanted to.

Now Dr. Carver was doing experiments with sweet potatoes. More and more farmers were growing sweet potatoes. They grew so many potatoes they could not sell them all. The potatoes they couldn't sell went to waste.

Dr. Carver had an idea. Sweet potatoes were good for eating — but if he could find more ways of using sweet potatoes, more sweet potatoes could be sold.

In his laboratory, Dr. Carver found that dozens of different and useful things could be made from the sweet potato — flour, starch, sugar, and molasses; vinegar, ink, dye, and glue. That was just the beginning. Before he was done, Dr. Carver had made over a hundred different products from the sweet potato. Now farmers could sell as many sweet potatoes as they could grow.

When news of Dr. Carver's experiments went out, he became famous all over the United States, and in other countries too.

Dr. Carver went on with his work. He began to do experiments with another plant that was good for the soil — the peanut. He wanted farmers to

When he was not busy in his laboratory, Dr. Carver liked to work in his greenhouse.

plant peanuts instead of cotton. In 1916, he wrote a booklet for farmers called "How to Grow the Peanut." In the booklet were recipes for a hundred and five different foods that could be made with peanuts.

The same year, some important scientists in England heard about Dr. Carver's experiments. The scientists belonged to the Royal Society of Arts, and they thought George Washington Carver should belong too. They voted him in. Dr. Carver became one of the few Americans to be a member of the famous Royal Society of Arts.

Seventeen

AT FOUR O'CLOCK every morning, Dr. Carver woke up. He climbed out of bed and got dressed in the dark. Then he left his rooms and walked to the woods. It was quiet and peaceful there — like a church.

"Nothing is more beautiful than the woods before sunrise," he told a friend. "At no other time have I so sharp an understanding of what God means to do with me. When other folks are still asleep, I hear God best and learn His plan."

On the way back to his laboratory every morning, Dr. Carver picked a flower to wear in his buttonhole. Then he went into his laboratory, locked the door, and put on his long canvas apron.

Dr. Carver was doing more experiments with peanuts. Many farmers had taken his advice and planted peanuts instead of cotton. But they could not sell all the peanuts they grew. They wanted to go back to growing cotton.

But to Dr. Carver, peanuts were so good for the soil and so good for people that he was not going to give up on them. He was trying to find more uses for them, just as he had done with the sweet potato. As he worked, he began to see that the peanut was going to be even more useful to man.

"The peanut will beat the sweet potato by far," he said.

For one thing, peanuts could be used to make many different foods. Dr. Carver had once made a whole dinner with peanuts — soup, mock chicken, a creamed vegetable, salad, cookies, ice cream, and coffee. None of Dr. Carver's guests knew the foods were made with peanuts until he told them.

Dr. Carver made a kind of milk from the peanut. Peanut milk could be made into cheese and buttermilk. He did more and more experiments. And when he was through, he had made over

Dr. Carver used chemistry to make new products out of the sweet potato and the peanut.

three hundred products from the peanut.

When Dr. Carver showed his peanut products, it was like a magic show. He pulled out bottles and jars filled with samples of his products — washing powder, bleach, shoe polish, metal polish, ink, rubbing oil and cooking oil, axle grease, cattle feeds, thirty different dyes, a kind of plastic, shampoo, soap, shaving cream. He even made linoleum and a kind of rubber from peanut shells.

When people heard what he had done, Dr. Carver was named The Wizard of Tuskegee. He could have been rich by selling his ideas to other people. But he let others use his ideas for nothing.

"What is money when I have all the earth?" he said.

Thomas Alva Edison, the famous inventor, asked Dr. Carver to come to Menlo Park and work for him. But Dr. Carver did not want to leave Tuskegee.

"If I were to go with you," he told Mr. Edison, "my work would not be known as mine, and my people would get no credit. I want my people to have the credit for whatever I may do."

Even though slavery had ended when Dr. Carver was a little boy, his people were not as free as white people. Blacks were not given equal rights, not even a famous man like George Washington Carver.

In some cities Dr. Carver could not stay in the best hotel, because the best hotel did not take blacks as guests. If he visited someone at the hotel, he would have to take the freight elevator or walk up the stairs.

In one city, Dr. Carver once saw some beautiful flowers in a park. He went into the park to touch them, but a guard stopped him on the way. "Get out of here, uncle," the guard said. "You know that colored people are not allowed in this park."

"They don't understand," Dr. Carver said to himself. "They don't understand." Then he went back to thinking about the work he had to do that day.

Eighteen

EVERY WEEK, the mailman left a big pile of mail for Dr. Carver. Some letters were from people who wanted him to give a speech. Whenever Dr. Carver spoke, all the seats in the hall were filled. Sometimes the people asked him what gave him the idea to do experiments with the peanut. He told this story:

One morning I was talking to God.

"Mr. Creator, what was the universe made for?" I asked Him.

"You want to know too much," He answered. "Your mind is too small to know that much."

Then I asked Him, "Mr. Creator, what was man made for?"

"Little man," He said, "you still want to know too much."

Then I asked Him to tell me about the peanut. "Mr. Creator, what is the peanut for?"

"That's more like it," He said.

Then I went into my laboratory and tried to find out what the peanut was and why God had made it.

In 1941, Dr. Carver gave a speech at his old school, Simpson College.

Many people who wrote to Dr. Carver wanted his help and advice. He tried to answer all the letters that came to him. He never asked anyone to pay him for his advice. If someone asked him about a special plant, Dr. Carver would not only tell the person all about the plant, he would also send him a packet of seeds and tell him how to grow the plant himself.

George Washington Carver lived alone. He had never married. When someone asked him why, he said, "I never had the time. Besides, what woman would want to live with a man who gets up at four o'clock in the morning — to talk to flowers?"

As Dr. Carver grew older, his hair grew white and then he began to get bald. He got up after sunrise now, and did not go walking alone in the woods so much. A housekeeper came to take care of him. She cleaned his rooms and cooked his meals.

Dr. Carver lived in two small rooms in a building where students lived too. Plants filled the windows. Bookcases full of books stood against every wall. In one case were hundreds of beautiful rocks that Dr. Carver had collected from all the places he had been. Some of the paintings he had done were hanging over the bookcases. Tables were covered with lace mats he had made.

In one corner was an old spinning wheel. This was the spinning wheel his mother had used. Dr. Carver had brought it back from Diamond Grove the last time he had gone there.

Every day Dr. Carver walked from his rooms to his new laboratory. There were young men to help him with his work, but he liked to work alone most of the time. Sometimes people came to Tuskegee just to see Dr. Carver working in his laboratory. He did not like to be stared at, but he was too polite to tell the people to go away.

In 1936, when George Washington Carver was seventy-two years old, Tuskegee held a celebration for him. It was his anniversary. He had been at Tuskegee for forty years. An artist was hired to make a statue of Dr. Carver for the celebration.

Dr. Carver did not like so much fuss. "I'm not ready to be a monument," he said. Dr. Carver had

Even when he was old, Dr. Carver took long walks in woods and fields, looking for unusual plants and flowers that he could study.

done everything he could to help his people, and that was what was important to him.

Dr. Carver had done more than help poor black farmers begin to have a better life. Because of his experiments, farming all over the South had changed.

More and more farmers were planting peanut crops instead of cotton. Peanuts became the sixth largest crop grown in the United States. Even cotton farmers were raising better cotton plants, thanks to George Washington Carver's experiments in growing cotton.

Now there were new uses for cotton too. Dr. Carver had found a way to use cotton as a kind of cushion in road pavement, and for wallboards that could be used instead of wood for building walls in houses.

Dr. Carver used chemistry to make new products out of plants. Today scientists use chemistry to make *synthetics* — products such as plastic and nylon. George Washington Carver was one of the first scientists to experiment with synthetics and to see how important they would be. He made a new kind of stone — a synthetic marble — out of wood shavings. And he made other synthetic products no one had thought of.

Our country honored George Washington Carver by putting his picture on a United States postage stamp. The stamp was issued in 1948.

When Dr. Carver was seventy-four years old, he became very sick. He thought he could cure himself by eating nothing but nature's food — wild lettuce, clover tops, dandelions, watercress, and other wild plants he had loved to eat all his life. But even when he was better, Dr. Carver was too weak to walk far, and he moved to rooms closer to his work.

Dr. Carver was working on plans for a museum that was going to be made at Tuskegee — the George Washington Carver Museum. There would be room in the museum for all the paintings he had done, all the lacework he had made. There would be samples of the paints he had made from clay, and of the products he had made from the sweet potato and the peanut.

While he was working on plans for the museum, Dr. Carver was invited to New York City by the President of the United States, Franklin D. Roosevelt. At a special dinner for George Washington Carver, the President gave him a medal. He thanked Dr. Carver for doing so much for his people, for science, and for the country.

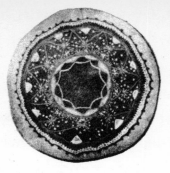

Dr. Carver made this mat.
First he crocheted it and then
he embroidered it.

Nineteen

Two years later, in 1941, the George Washington Carver Museum was opened. People from all over the United States and from Europe came to see it. They were surprised when they came into the room full of paintings and lacework. They knew Dr. Carver was a great scientist, but they didn't know he was an artist too.

All the paintings Dr. Carver had done when he went to art school were there— pictures of roses, of pond lilies, of wild orchids growing on a fence. And there were other pictures done with paints

Dr. Carver had made from Alabama clay. He had painted them during the years he had been at Tuskegee.

One of the most beautiful things in the museum was not a painting. Dr. Carver had put together all the little wood shapes he had whittled when he was a boy. There were over a thousand of them, and he had joined them all together — without glue, or string, or nails — to make a design.

This design was put into a picture frame and hung in the museum. Every time Dr. Carver looked at it he remembered the years when he was a little boy. How long ago they were! How much had changed since then. How much had changed because of him.

George Washington Carver died early in the morning of January 5, 1943. He was seventy-nine years old. He had lived his life to help others, and that is the best a person can do.